the way we wore

black style then

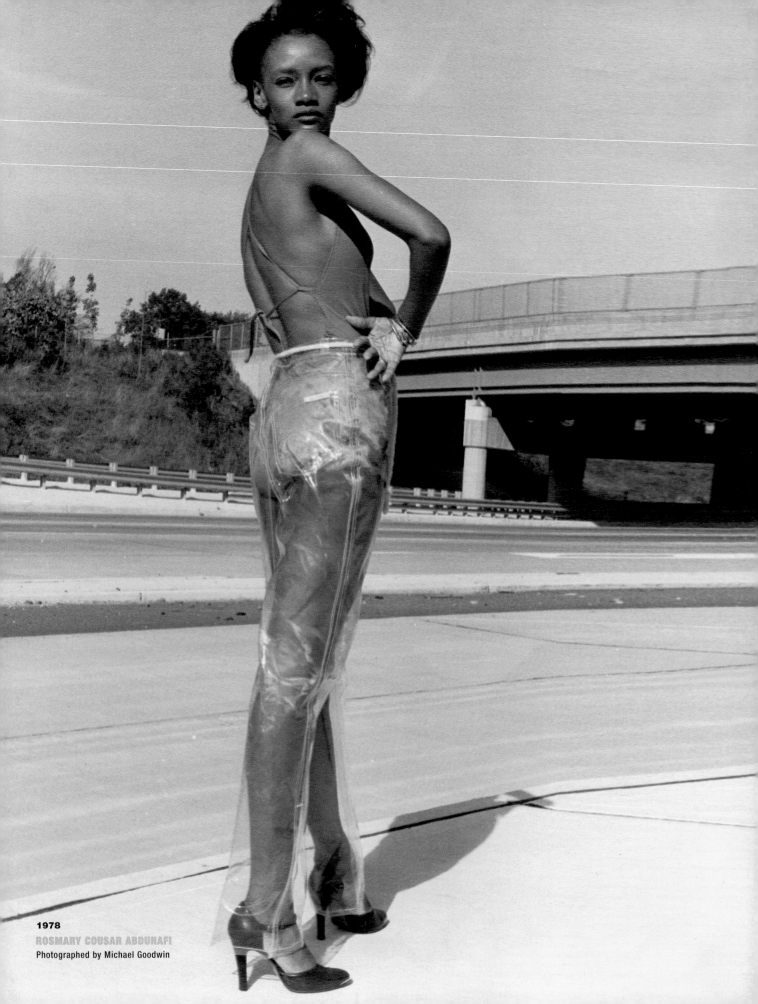

1978
ROSMARY COUSAR ABDUNAFI
Photographed by Michael Goodwin

the way we wore

black style then

michael mccollom

foreword by **GEOFFREY HOLDER** creative director **RENEE HUNTER**

Glitterati
INCORPORATED

NEW YORK, NEW YORK

Special Thanks

Renee Hunter, we did what we did and we got what we got! Luv Ya!
Geoffrey Holder thank you for always being an inspiration to me and the world,
Henry McCollom, Richard Bradley, Douglas Says…, Steven Robinson, Michael
Henry Adams thanks for BLACK STYLE NOW, Phyllis Swan-Rankin, Kevin Shaprio,
Sharon"Magic"Jordon, Stanley & Jane Blum, Renaldo Barnette, Michael Butler,
Daniel Dease, Ben Cassara, Kenn Duncan, Daniel Green, Purmoi Gordenot, Julie Skarratt,
Chris Green, Michael Goodwin, Marta Hallett & Glitterati, Nancy Leonard, and an
extra special thanks to all the fabulous participants who so graciously granted
permissions to share their stylish photographic moments in *The Way We Wore*.

First published in the United States of America in 2006 by Glitterati Incorporated
225 Central Park West, New York, New York 10024
Telephone 212 362 9119/Fax 212 362 7174
www.Glitteratiincorporated.com

First edition, 2006

Library of Congress Control Number: 2006925131

Hardcover ISBN 0-9777531-1-5

Design by Nancy Leonard

Printed and bound in China by Hong Kong Graphics & Printing Ltd.

10 9 8 7 6 5 4 3 2 1

Dedicated To

Albertha & Henry McCollom
  (mom & pops)
Thank you for giving me the freedom to fly!

—*Michael*

Contents

The Way We Wore

One should not enter a room and expect ambiance; one should enter and become it.

Those that grace the pages of *The Way We Wore* took that concept and ran with it. Though the reader will witness the evolution—and, in some cases, the faux pas—of fashion and design, it is the personal flair that an individual bestows to each outfit that creates the look.

Michael McCollom has put together a collection of never-before-seen photographs of the individual. *The Way We Wore* is not only a historical piece that journeys through the African-American landscape, but is also an album celebrating the individual. Like a yearbook, you will come back to this work again and again. Though you may not know the people personally, you will recognize them. Michael has carefully chosen pictures and people that exhibit the historical framework of African-American influence on fashion, design, and culture.

The book takes an exceptional look back at style moments and, in doing so, explores the beginnings of a diverse group of African-American tastemakers, some of whom literally "pulled it together." No matter what the achieved look, though, these were individuals in a time when fashion was bold. Fashion now is far too relaxed, with no formality, no rules. Though some of these looks may be considered conventional, while others outrageous, the clothing never overpowered the wearer; it enhanced, never dictated.

Most importantly, Michael has put together a book that subscribes to the notion that style can be expressed in dress, gesture, or attitude. Be bold, take risks, and experiment!

GEOFFREY HOLDER
New York City

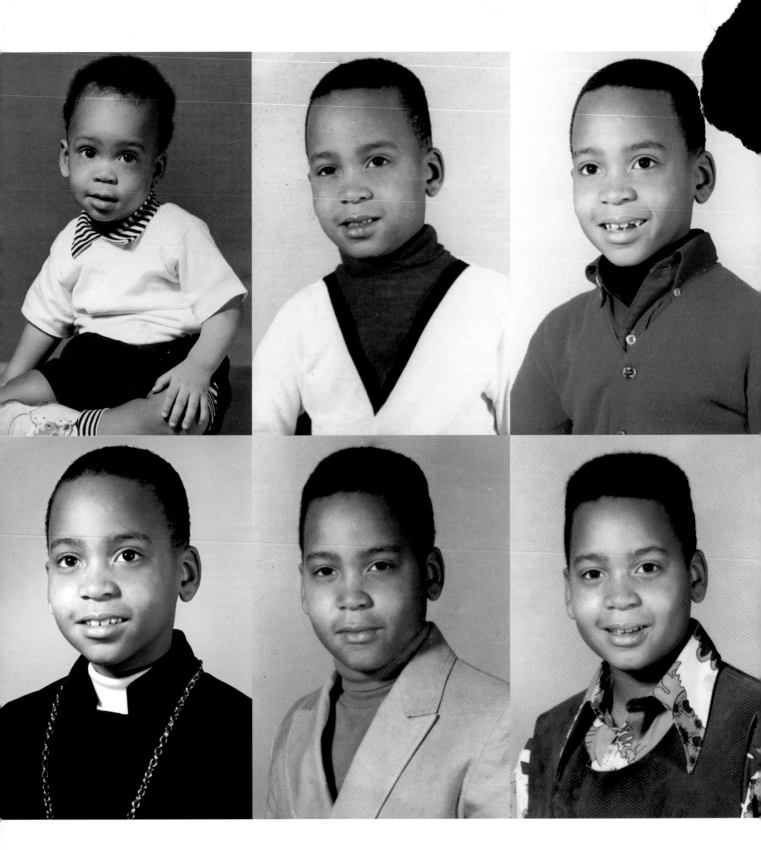

Introduction

As far back as I can remember I have always had a love of fashion.

All fashion: the good, the bad, and the awful. Fashion in my opinion has always been less about clothes (even though my chosen profession is that of designer) and more about style & attitude. For me style has always been far more democratic than fashion. I was born in the 60's and my family was very Black middle class. Our mode of living was not extravagant, but we lived life extravagantly through our style. Early on I was inundated with style, from my mother's ever evolving looks, to my grandmothers steadfast devotion to her Chanel influenced Kimberly Knit suits. For us back to school shopping took on the importance of the couture shows of Paris. My mother would pre-shop the stores for trends and direction, put items on hold for us and then we would go in for fittings. If we liked a certain style particularly well, say a shirt or pants, she would not just buy us the one but one in every colorway or pattern. Clothing had importance for us; an importance not dictated by a designer label, it was more about what you wanted to wear and when to wear it. We had outfits for school. We had outfits for picnics. We had outfits for church. We had outfits for holidays.

My parents were very social. I would sit in anticipation to see my mom's new formal dress, or which of my dad's tuxedos would be chosen for the evening. Yes he had more than one, he had several from a 60's Sutach-embroidered shawl collared style to a 70's Cranberry velvet two-button with grosgrain trim (think Tom Ford's Gucci collection fall 1999). Dad too was always dapper and the epitome of fashion. The unexpected was a given in our house and change was an imperative.

This evolution is very apparent in my grade school photos. Kindergarten - 5TH from Star Trek to Layered Prep, Nehru to Hippie my changing style was celebrated never discouraged. I recently discovered this early rebellious celebration of style not to be uncommon among my peers in fashion. This revelation was the genesis of this photographic journey.

I invited over 100 fashion insiders, outsiders, and beautiful people to share their personal photos. Style is so subjective, if you ask 100 people what style is, you'll get 100 different points of view. The result of their submissions, *The Way We Wore: Black Style Then* a unique review of fashion and moreover personal style.

MICHAEL McCOLLOM

"Fashions fade, style is eternal."

YVES SAINT LAURENT

1977 ▪ Cincinnati, Ohio

WOODWARD HIGH SCHOOL HOMECOMING DANCE

"By this time, at age seventeen, I was completely seduced by Vogue and GQ. Velvet double-breasted blazer, polyester shirt and slacks, and a silk pocket hanky: oh so very Studio 54 (or at least I thought I was)! That's Renee Wright behind the chair, and Teresa Chambers to my left. From the smile on my face, this photo must have been taken before I found out I had lost the title of Mr. Woodward 1978. It was a very Carrie moment for me, sans the pig's blood!"

MICHAEL McCOLLOM

1986 ▪ New York City

"Okay, this is one of those bad style decisions. I was still very cutting-edge; this photo was taken five years before Milli Vanilli appeared on the scene."

MICHAEL McCOLLOM

1985 ▪ Edinburgh, Scotland

"I am wearing full Scottish formal gear, including a kilt, at a dinner party in Edinburgh Castle."

GEORGE CODRINGTON PRYCE JR.
Publicist

1941 ▪ Cincinnati, Ohio

"My mother, Albertha McCollom, had this portrait taken shortly
after arriving in Cincinnati from Baton Rouge, Louisiana. She had
just turned twenty years old. In this photo she is wearing her first
(but not last) fur coat, a birthday gift from my grandmother."

MICHAEL McCOLLOM

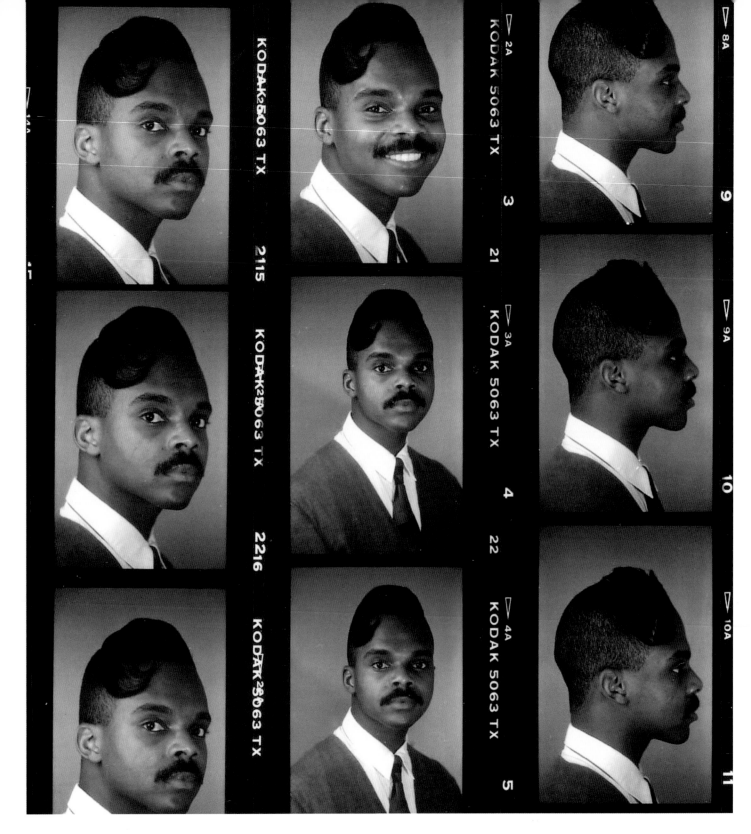

1990 ■ New York City

"I wanted hair. My friend David Stockdale gave it to me. I wore
it to my first Seventh Avenue fashion show at ISAIA NYC."

RICHARD BRADLEY Regional Retail Manager

Right:

Late 60's
Cincinnati, Ohio
"Here's my sister, La Verne Corbin; even though she thought she had skinny legs, she loved mini-dresses in the 60's and 70's."
MICHAEL McCOLLOM

Opposite page:

Easter, 1974
Hollywood, Florida
SUNDAY BEST
"Easter was always a time to look your best, for church. My mom often bought us matching dresses. My sister did not want to wear the hat, as you can see. When I see this photo, I think I had no choice but to become a model. That's me on the left, my sister Nichole Renee Sierra, and my mom Hattie E. Sierra."
LU CELANIA SIERRA
Model/Actress

Left:

1970 ▪ Brooklyn, New York

"Here I am with a friend, hanging out at the Tip Top Bar on Fulton Street."

BERNARD J. MARSH (R)
Actor/Choreographer/Director

Right:

1940's ▪ Philadelphia, Pennsylvania

"While searching through our family photo albums, I ran across this photo of my first cousin Archie Sweet. He's so debonair in his zoot suit, I knew he had to be included in The Way We Wore."

HENRY McCOLLOM

**May 1972 ▪ Durham,
North Carolina**
COLLEGE HOMECOMING
"I designed and made this
dress, added the accessories,
and snap—look just like a
queen! I loved this, all that
abstract design—it was
yellow and black in color."
EDNA-JAKKIE MILLER
Entrepreneur

Opposite page:

1970's ▪ New York City
FREDERICK S. SIMPSON
Retired Men's and Women's
Wear Designer

April 1959 ■ New York City
EASTER SUNDAY
ARLENE HAWKINS
Owner of Arlene Hawkins
Cosmetics

Left:

1968 ▪ New York City
TEST SHOOT
"Here I am trying to be
a print model."

BETHANN HARDISON
Talent Manager/Producer/
Documentarian

Right:

1970's ▪ Paris, France
"Andre Leon Talley and I
are in the street, on our
way to a party."

BETHANN HARDISON
Talent Manager/Producer/
Documentarian

June 1962
PROM

"I'm at my cousin Kim's house for her prom. Her dress is my own design (of course)."

TRACY REESE (L)
Fashion Designer

1992 ▪ New York City
MAGASCHONI SHOWROOM
"My hat!"

TRACY REESE
Fashion Designer

"With hair, heels, and attitude, honey, I am through the roof."

RU PAUL

1963
Harlem, New York
"Here are the club members at our HAT cocktail party. That's me on the far right, in the long leather gloves."
NAOMI INGRAM

1990 ▪ Mahattan, New York

"This was a party for hairstylist Rudy Townsell. I'm in the center with platinum blond barrel curls by James Harris. That's Coco Mitchell to my left, and Portia La Beija at my right."

SHARON "MAGIC" JORDAN
Model/Minister/Mom

GEORGE DANDY (L) AND
ALFRED MURPHY (R)

1968 ■ St. Louis, Missouri
EMMA DAVIS (L)
GLADYS BRADLEY (R)

1989 ▪ Paris, France

"This series of photos was taken at a party after Patrick Kelly's Fall/Winter Collection at Regines. Iman and I walked in the show. At the time, we could not have imagined it would be his last collection. What can I say? Patrick was wonderful!"

SHARON "MAGIC" JORDAN
Model/Minister/Mom

POOL PARTY

"The theme was Sodom
and Gomorrah, and we were
asked to wear gold or white.
I thought that white would
look like drawers, so I
opted for gold. It was one
decadent night."

SEAN JACKSON
Graphic Designer

1954 ▪ Harlem, New York
"This photo of my aunt, Dorothy Dickerson, was taken on the rooftop of Harlem Hospital. She moved from Cincinnati to New York to attend nursing school there. Here she looks to be catching some rays (or maybe the eye of a young doctor) during a much-needed break between classes."

MICHAEL McCOLLOM

Early 80's ▪ East Village, New York

"I'm in the Greenwich Village apartment of my then kingman (boyfriend) now husband Denrick Cooper, overlooking Tompkins Square. We're dressed like this because of our Rastafarian faith. I'm wearing the colors that reflect black pride, African unity, and Rasta: the colors in the flags of several African countries. Of course, it's a long dress. I'm still really good at tying turbans, although I don't wear them much anymore.

"We were dressed to go out, although my outfit here is not unusual for me. If he were in his typical day outfit, he'd look a lot more like what most people picture a Rasta man wearing; that is, like Bob Marley. It would be very casual: maybe a military shirt, a knit vest, cotton pants and a tam. Instead, here he's wearing more of that rude-boy, ska style that developed out of ska and reggae, and was celebrated by artists like Gregory Isaacs and Barrington Levy. We were going out to eat: definitely Indian because we were vegetarian. Well, he still is. You could feel like you were really having a night out at the Indian restaurants in the village without spending a lot of money, which we didn't have. So it was a big deal."

CONSTANCE C.R. WHITE
Author/Fashion Journalist

1968 ■ New York City

"This was a test shoot with pal Robert Freeman. I'm wearing a monkey-fur vest, which I found in a vintage shop. So fabulous!"

RENEE HUNTER
Entrepeneur

1980 ▪ Boston, Massachusetts

"Looks like I'm prepared for a night on the town."

REGINALD VAN LEE
Management Consultant

1955 ▪ Harlem, New York
BUTLER STUDIOS WEDDING PORTRAIT

JAMES AND NAOMI INGRAM

September 16, 1967 ▪ Jersey City, New Jersey
WEDDING DAY

MRS. GLORIA WATFORD AND HER PARENTS
CORNELIUS AND GLORIA ROBINSON

May 28, 1969 ■ New York City

"This is on my wedding day, at Barbetta's on West 46th Street. I'm wearing Edie Gladstone for Debs: a white cotton lace dress, white satin ribbon, and made-to-order scarf. The white leather heels are Florentinas, and the gloves are by Roger Ferre… all topped off with an 8mm pearl necklace and a violet bouquet!"

AUDREY SMALTZ
Founder/CEO of The Ground Crew

1965 ■ New York City

"Always a bridal model…
never a bride!"

RENEE HUNTER
Entrepreneur

1981 ▪ Detroit, Michigan

"We were on our way to Easter Sunday service. It goes without saying that we had to get all decked out. The most memorable thing about this photo to me is the fact that as an eight-year-old child, I was wearing my sixty-one-year-old father's hat. This picture is so true of the relationship between my cousin Levie Darnell McIlwain and me. I was always very introverted and subdued, and he was always (and still is) the loud, outgoing one. Those differences aside, we are still like brothers today. When we were younger, he was always the better dresser, but I grew into my own and now give him style advice."

AARON MARQUE POTTS (R)

Designer

1952 ▪ Wichita Falls, Texas
SHEPARD AIR FORCE BASE
"Here my dad, Henry McCollom
(right), and a pal are looking to
meet 'nice' girls at the USO club."
MICHAEL McCOLLOM

1967 ▪ Chicago, Illinois

"Velvet dinner jackets, tuxedos and dress suits were all the rage, That's Stanley Hilton in a black single-breasted tuxedo with a velvet ruff (tie). I'm wearing a lightweight black velvet dinner jacket with a white satin Russian Cossack shirt. Richard Brown wears a Victorian evening suit of gunmetal-gray velvet, and Raoul Hilton is on the right in a double-breasted black tuxedo with mother-of-pearl buttons and a conventional bowtie."

GEORGE CODRINGTON PRYCE JR.
Publicist

"I was privileged to be a make-up artist on this unbelievable photo shoot: Naomi Campbell, Tyra Banks, Iman, and Beverly Johnson—all the top black supermodels—together for Iman's book *I Am Iman*. The photographer was Annie Leibovitz. I snapped this candid shot between set-ups, and as you can see everyone was having a wonderful time."

BYRON BARNES
Make-up Artist

1971 ▪ Orlando, Florida
CARVER JUNIOR
HIGH SCHOOL
"I'm at the pre-homecoming
game, in twin mode with
my sister Sylvia."

SHARON "MAGIC" JORDAN
Model/Minister/Mom

1974 ▪ Cincinnati, Ohio
JAZZ FESTIVAL
PAMELA CRENSHAW
AND DARLENE STONE

1970 ▪ Stockholm, Sweden
SAILING
WILLIAM AND BARBARA TATUM

1960's ▪ Cincinnati, Ohio

"Here are William and Catherine McCollom, my forever cool Uncle Bill and Aunt Ann. They lived in Cleveland, where he owned a hair salon called Magic Shears. When they would come to visit it was always a fashion moment for me. Here Uncle Bill is in full 'Rat Pack' mode, and Aunt Ann is very chic and understated, as always. (For the record before Ann there was Aunt Melvina and later Aunt Roz.... but hey that's another book!)"

MICHAEL McCOLLOM

"I adore that pink! It's the navy blue of India!"

DIANA VREELAND

1994 ▪ New York City
"We're celebrating the
birthday of my mother
Ruth Barnes at the
Rhiga Royal Hotel."
BYRON BARNES
Make-up Artist

1974 ■ Cincinnati, Ohio

"Think pink! I was forever in awe of my big brother, Ricky Corbin, with his creative sense of style. As quiet as he is, he always made bold fashion statements. Prom night 1974 was no exception; here is with his date, Pam Miller, wearing a pink and white paisley jacquard tuxedo jacket, bright pink ruffle shirt, and our dad's red and black polka-dot cummerbund."

MICHAEL McCOLLOM

Left:

November 1980 ▪ Dallas, Texas

BISHOP LYNCH HIGH SCHOOL HOMECOMING

"Wow, it's so long ago… my first homecoming dance with my first girlfriend, Missy Robinson. I think we were the only African-American couple at the dance (it was a predominantly white school). You couldn't tell us anything; we thought we were 'stylin'! Of course, I look back now and wonder what I was thinking, and where all the hair has gone! And I'm sure Missy is totally embarrassed about her shoes."

DERRICK THOMPSON
Vice President, Music Publishing

Right:

1978 ▪ Cincinnati, Ohio

WOODWARD HIGH SCHOOL SENIOR PROM

"Sonya Sinkfield-Dixon, my best friend from high school, only agreed to give me this photo if I would remove her date from the picture. So I did! I loved her dress; she made it herself from a Vogue Designer Pattern by Diane von Furstenberg. This in itself would not have been unique, except for the fact that the pattern was originally for a nightgown. She created it, in true 70's fashion, using Quiana fabric in a champagne color. It's belted with a gold metal snake belt, but her date's hand (the only thing left of him!) conceals that detail. Even more unconventional, she completed the look with a pair of ultra-flat Calvin Klein sandals: very sophisticated for a seventeen-year-old."

MICHAEL McCOLLOM

1978 ▪ Cincinnati, Ohio
WOODWARD HIGH
SCHOOL SENIOR PROM
"I designed the ivory raw silk
two-button blazer I'm wearing, and begged my dad for
about a month to give me the
money to purchase these
ivory/cream cap toe Bally
of Switzerland shoes. The
surprising back story to this
photo is, she wasn't my prom
date! My real date's dress did
not coordinate as well with
my look; it was, shall we say,
a bit more of the times. I
thought Denise Harris's taupe
column dress would be more
timeless and classic, so
we posed together for this
one when her boyfriend
wasn't looking."

MICHAEL McCOLLOM

May 1983 ▪ Paramus, New Jersey
DICKINSON HIGH SCHOOL SENIOR PROM

"I was really nervous about my date Evelyn Cologne's dress. It was a bit over-the-top for that time, but she was the type of girl who loved the attention... and so did I. As for myself, I think simple black tie would have sufficed. And that shag haircut! What was I thinking?"

STEVEN J. ROBINSON
Creative Director

1977 ▪ Cincinnati, Ohio
BEVERLY HILLS SUPPER CLUB

"Kahron Gibson and I were three years old when she moved
to my block, and we've been inseparable ever since. I snapped
this photo at her senior prom. For Kahron, this was a perfect
night. Her date for the evening was Damon Lynch III, her high
school crush."

MICHAEL McCOLLOM

1970's ▪ Italy

"This wool herringbone cape with matching trousers was by Eric Lund, for the Norcissa-New York Boutique, which I owned."

GWEN MAZER *Personal Style Consultant*
Photographed by Purmol Gordenot

1968 ▪ Cincinnati, Ohio
THE MOTOWN LOOK
RICHARD BRADLEY SR.

1978 ▪ Newark,
New Jersey
LINWOOD ALLEN
Designer

1960's ▪ Boston,
Massachusetts
R. ASHTON WALL
Writer

1960's ■ New York City
CENTRAL PARK
"Long before Donyale, Naomi
S., Naomi C., Beverly J., and
all the others, there was me!"
DON MARTIN
Semi-Retired Dance Teacher

Opposite page:

1982 ▪ New York City
FIFTH AVENUE

LLOYD WILLIAMS
Designer

Left:

1964 ▪ Paris, France
AMAZING!

**GEOFFREY HOLDER AND
CARMEN DE LAVALLADE**

1980's ■ New York City
COURTNEY PERRY
Visual Director

May 1960 ▪ New York City
ARLENE HAWKINS
Owner of Arlene Hawkins
Cosmetics

1987 ▪ New York City

"Either I am receiving a hug or being accosted by hat designer Ray Hands at Milk Bar."

PHYLLIS SWAN-RANKIN
Beautiful Entrepreneur

1989 ▪ New York City
"Here I am channeling 'Madge Wildwood,' with a dash of CHANEL at a friend's wedding with model Colin."
PHYLLIS SWAN-RANKIN
Beautiful Entrepreneur

"Hair has always been important."

DIANA ROSS

Opposite Page:

1988 ▪ New York City
"This photo is an outtake
from headshots taken for my
fashion column, 'Retail Rap,'
which ran in the New York
Post from 1988 until 1993. I
love it because it features
some of my favorite designers
of the time: Tahari jacket,
Robert Lee Morris pin, my
sister Jensen's gold leaf and
glass marble earrings, my
beloved Patrick Kelly baby pin,
which got cropped in the final
photo… and dig the hair!"
PATRICIA JACOBS
Journalist/Artist

Left:

1966 ■ New York City
"I was in art school at the time; just a happy-go-lucky teen."
CHARLES D. SNUGGS
Make-up Artist

Right:

September 1967
"This was taken at Ferdinan Suchmadaser Elementary School. I couldn't get the hair on the sides of my head to form an afro. Undoubtedly, I've never spent as much time in the open air as I did when I was eleven years old… so I've never since been so thin and tan. I wanted a Nehru jacket, but my father said he'd get me one when I was sixteen. By 1972 they were passé. Still, with my jaunty kerchief, I thought I looked good."
MICHAEL HENRY ADAMS
Historian

"What a difference a
year makes... the afro!"

VERONICA JONES
Boutique Owner

1975 ▪ Chattanooga, Tennessee
GARY LAMPLEY

1973 ▪ Shaker Heights, Ohio
CHERYL LEWIS-FLEMING

1973 ▪ Cincinnati, Ohio

LINDA GOODWIN

1974 ▪ Cincinnati, Ohio

RICHARD CORBIN

1976 ■ Harlem, New York

"During the70's and into the early 80's, I wore my hair in an afro. For whatever reason, this photograph was taken with black-and-white film, but I remember the colors. Vividly. The skirt, a cotton wrap-around, was royal blue with chevron stripes of white and red. The one-piece blue-sleeved body suit comple-mented the skirt. But it was the boots—royal blue with white piping—that brought this outfit together. They were hard to miss. I loved those boots! But alas, one could only wear so many outfits with them. Oh, memory."

LANA TURNER
Licensed Real Estate
Salesperson

1972 ▪ New York City
CENTRAL PARK

VY HIGGINSEN
Radio Personality/
Producer/Writer

"Express yourself,
don't repress yourself."

MADONNA

July 6, 1958 ▪ Port Jarvus, New York

KING'S LODGE AT SALLY'S PARADISE FARMS

"Left to right, it's Alice Arrington, Frances Armstead, Marlene
Turner, myself, Alice, Vivian Joseph and Adelle, on the beach
at The Colored Resort."

AUDREY SMALTZ Founder/CEO of The Ground Crew

1993 ▪ Queens, New York
RIIS BEACH WHITE PARTY

"Here's me with Moi Renee (center) and Joseph Bogain (right).
It was Ralph's annual birthday party on Riis Beach. The color
that year was white. Although no one believed me, my swimsuit
(unlike Moi Renee's) was men's! It was a Nikos bodysuit I bought
while on vacation on Germany on the isle of Sylt. I still have it."
RICHARD BRADLEY

I-GO-4U

1967 ▪ Young Island, West Indies

"I'm sunning on a private island paradise near St. Vincent in the Caribbean Grenadines, West Indies."

GWEN MAZER
Personal Style Consultant

1979, ▪ Rio de Janeiro
IPANEMA BEACH
BETHANN HARDISON
Talent Manager/Producer/
Documentarian

1989 ▪ Cancun, Mexico
MARGO TURNQUEST-LEWIS
Event Production Designer

June 1972
Brooklyn, New York
"This was at a high school
graduation party, at a
friend's house."

EARL-RODNEY HOLMAN
Merchandise Consultant

1990 ▪ New York City

"This photo was taken at a cocktail party on West 72nd in Manhattan for Michael McCollom after his debut collection for ISAIA. Of course I am wearing a look straight off the runway, including a raw crystal cross necklace design by Ron Anderson at the start of his jewelry collection, Ten Thousand Things."

PORTIA LABEIJA
Legendary Socialite
Photographed by Ben Cassara

"Stumbling is not falling."

MALCOLM X

1990's ■ New York City

"Jody Whatley, Madonna and British fashion were all the
rage. The first M.A.C. make-up store had just opened up in
the village—my favorite lipstick shade was Russian Red.
Can you tell?"

MONTGOMERY HARRIS Fashion Designer

1991 ▪ New York City
BEATNIK IN THE VILLAGE
"I'm on the corner of Christopher Street and Seventh Avenue on the way to meet "the gals" for brunch. Note the velvet vest over the jacket, the exaggerated shoulder and the John Lennon glasses. The motorcycle pouf hat added the extra *oomph*... or at least I thought so!"

BRUCE BOWENS
Designer

1989
BELINDA AND
EDWARD WILKERSON
Photographed by Daniel Dease

1983

"This was definitely my
black Madonna moment.
The flat granny boots are
pretty modern, if I do say
so myself!"

MICHAELA ANGELA DAVIS
Photographed by Chris Green

1984 ▪ Columbus, Missouri

"My fashion crew and I were looking for a great place to do a quick photo shoot and not be disturbed... need I say more?"

LAURITA SHIELDS
Fashion Stylist

1989

"This photo is of me and my best friend Karonda McKnight (right), on her sixteenth birthday."

SONYA MAGETT

1986 ▪ Brooklyn, New York

"This photo was shot in my apartment, prior to going out for an evening at the Palladium nightclub."

MICHAEL ASENDIO
Accessory Designer

1987 ▪ New York City
"Out clubbin' with friends!"
CONNIE "MILAN" KEARSE
Model/Actress

1981 ▪ Cincinnati, Ohio

"Going out with friends Melvin Wells (rear)
and Kevin Riser (right), disco dancing."

DARNELL BREWSTER Marketing Consultant

Right:

1985 ▪ **Rochelle,
New Jersey**
DOUGLAS SAYS...
Designer

"I always knew I was destined for greatness."

OPRAH WINFREY

1963 ■ Germany

"We were living in Germany; I was three years old and already particular about what to wear. I was MAD for corduroy and bucks!"

RENALDO A. BARNETTE
Fashion Designer

1987-1993

"I've always believed that the best accessory of a well dressed man is a beautiful woman! From the top, these are Tyra Banks, Coco Mitchell, and Kimora Lee Simmons."

RENALDO A. BARNETTE
Fashion Designer

1973-1976

Cincinnati, Ohio

"My school photos from first to third grade. I always picked out my own outfit. While there was a disco moment, I pretty much kept it traditional and classic."

EMIL WILBEKIN
Lifestyle and Culture
Expert/Journalist.

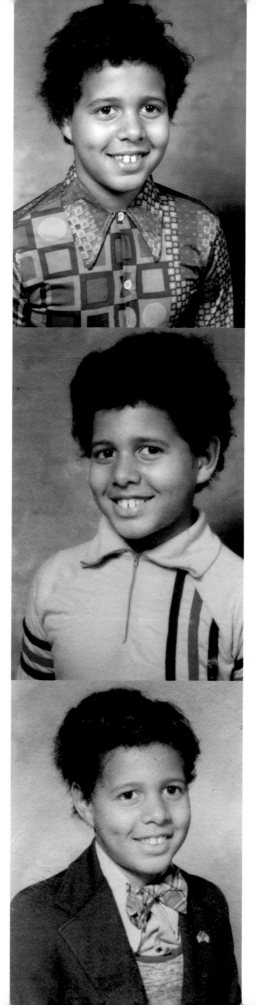

1963 ▪ Harlem, New York

"I'm standing outside my grandparents' apartment building on 137th street."

MARK INGRAM
Retail Store Ower

1970's
JAMES THOMPSON
Broadcast Entertainment
MBA Executive

1976
Barbados, West Indies
BABATU SPARROW
Designer

Left:

**1974 ▪ Jersey City,
New Jersey**
CHARLES BOYD
Interior Designer

Right:

1991 ▪ New York City
CHARLES BOYD
Interior Designer

1960 ▪ Birmingham, Alabama

"Easter was a true fashion moment for me, dressed from head to toe: bonnet, bow, and lots of frills."

MONTGOMERY HARRIS
Fashion Designer

1961 ▪ Cincinnati, Ohio
"Linda Goodwin, my sister...
prim and proper. When this
photo was taken, I think she
was about seven. I love this
shot because my mom added
on her thick ponytail hair-
piece. In my family it was
all about 'the look,' even at
age seven!"
MICHAEL McCOLLOM

1974 ■ Boston, MA

Sitting in between my older twin brothers Michael and Paul
Simpson for a 'Sunday Best' photo shoot. I guess I stood out
in my loud plaid jacket and bright socks… maybe a sign that
I was a fashion rebel at an early age."

MARK SIMPSON Designer

1940's ■ Brooklyn, New York
BED-STY GARDEN
REGINA, MICHAEL,
AND RENEE HUNTER

Opposite page:

1977 ▪ New York City
MICHAEL S. BUTLER
Fashion Designer

This page:

1986 ▪ New York City
PARADISE GARAGE
MEMBERSHIP CARD
MICHAEL S. BUTLER
Fashion Designer

"Be black, shine, aim high."

LEONTYNE PRICE

Opposite Page:

2001 ▪ New York City
EDWARD WILKERSON
Designer/Photographer

This page:

**Fall 1986 ▪ Newark,
New Jersey**
"I thought I was really carrying
on in this photo, dressed in
red and black satin by Kilgore
& Sweet, at a fashion show
dinner dance on a Saturday
evening. I'd done my own
make-up practically in the
dark, so in my mind my face
was beat to perfection."
JOYCE HANCOCK
Fashion Show Commentator,
"The Lady with the Golden Voice"

1979 ▪ Syracuse, New York
SYRACUSE UNIVERSITY
"I'm wearing a friend's fur
jacket after a dinner party."
DANIEL DEASE
Photographer

This page:

1970's ▪ Paris, France
"Designing my first
Spring/Summer couture line
for the house of Jean Louis
Scherrer, I got a call from the
White House! First Lady "Lady
Bird" Johnson was calling
to congratulate me for being
the first African-American
designer to do haute couture
in France."
JAY JAXON
Fashion Designer

September 2004

JUNE HORNE Senior Buyer, Retail

1982 ▪ Los Angeles,
California
BIRTHDAY STRIPPER

MARLENE CLARK
Retired Actress

1970s

"Taking a stroll in Laurel Canyon."

DON MARTIN
Semi-Retired Dance Teacher

1986 ▪ Austin, Texas

"Taking in the sights on 6th Street."

T. MYCHAEL RAMBO,
Actor/Singer

1970's ▪ New York City

"Here I am with Harvey
McLamore (center) and
James Diamond (right)"

RUFUS BARKLEY
Designer

1990 ▪ Atlanta, Georgia
**BONNER BROTHERS
HAIR SHOW**
"Yes, I'm wearing a hat
at a hair show!"

JOYCE GIBSON
Hair Stylist

1952
Montgomery, Alabama
"High school days…
I'm the one in the tie."
DR. ROBERT BREWSTER

Right:

1970's ▪ Cincinnati, Ohio
"This is my cousin, Damita (Joey) Flack. She would sew all my samples for me when I started designing in high school. She was (and still is) very creative and would bring my dreams and ideas to life. Here she is wearing one of her own creations. Check out the windowpane fishnet stockings!"
MICHAEL McCOLLOM

Opposite page:

1976 ▪ Trinidad, West Indies
ALVIN CLAYTON FERNANDEZ,
Artist/Model

Opposite page:

1950
HAL FREDERICK
Actor

This page:

1979
"Here I am with author
James Baldwin."
HAL FREDERICK
Actor

1971 ▪ New York City

"Here I am with the
Supremes, Jean Terrell (left)
and Mary Wilson (right)."

MICHAEL HURRELL
Costume, Designer

Left:

Christmas 1985
Massachusetts

My mother Josephine Premice
and I are celebrating the
holidays at a friend's home.
Mother is wearing Maison
Worth of Paris, and I am in
Stephen Burrows."

SUSAN FALES-HILL

Right:

2002 ▪ New York City

"Truly timeless: my mother's
Worth of Paris evening dress!"

SUSAN FALES-HILL
Photographed by Julie Skarratt

The Participants